GALLANTLY FOUGHT
THE QUEEN

GALLANTLY FOUGHT THE QUEEN

V Balakrishnan

ZERO DEGREE PUBLISHING

Title: Gallantly Fought the Queen
Author's name: V Balakrishnan
Copyright © V Balakrishnan 2023
Published By: Zero Degree Publishing

Zero Degree Publishing
No. 55(7), R Block, 6th Avenue,
Anna Nagar West,
Chennai - 600040
Ph: 8925061999

E mail: zerodegreepublishing@gmail.com
Website: www. zerodegreepublishing.com

First Edition by Zero Degree Publishing: March 2023
ISBN: 978-93-95233-02-6
ZDP Title: 55

Cover Design: Meera Sitaraman
Cover Photo: C Vishwajith

Typeset: Vidhya Velayudham
Printed at Clictoprint, India

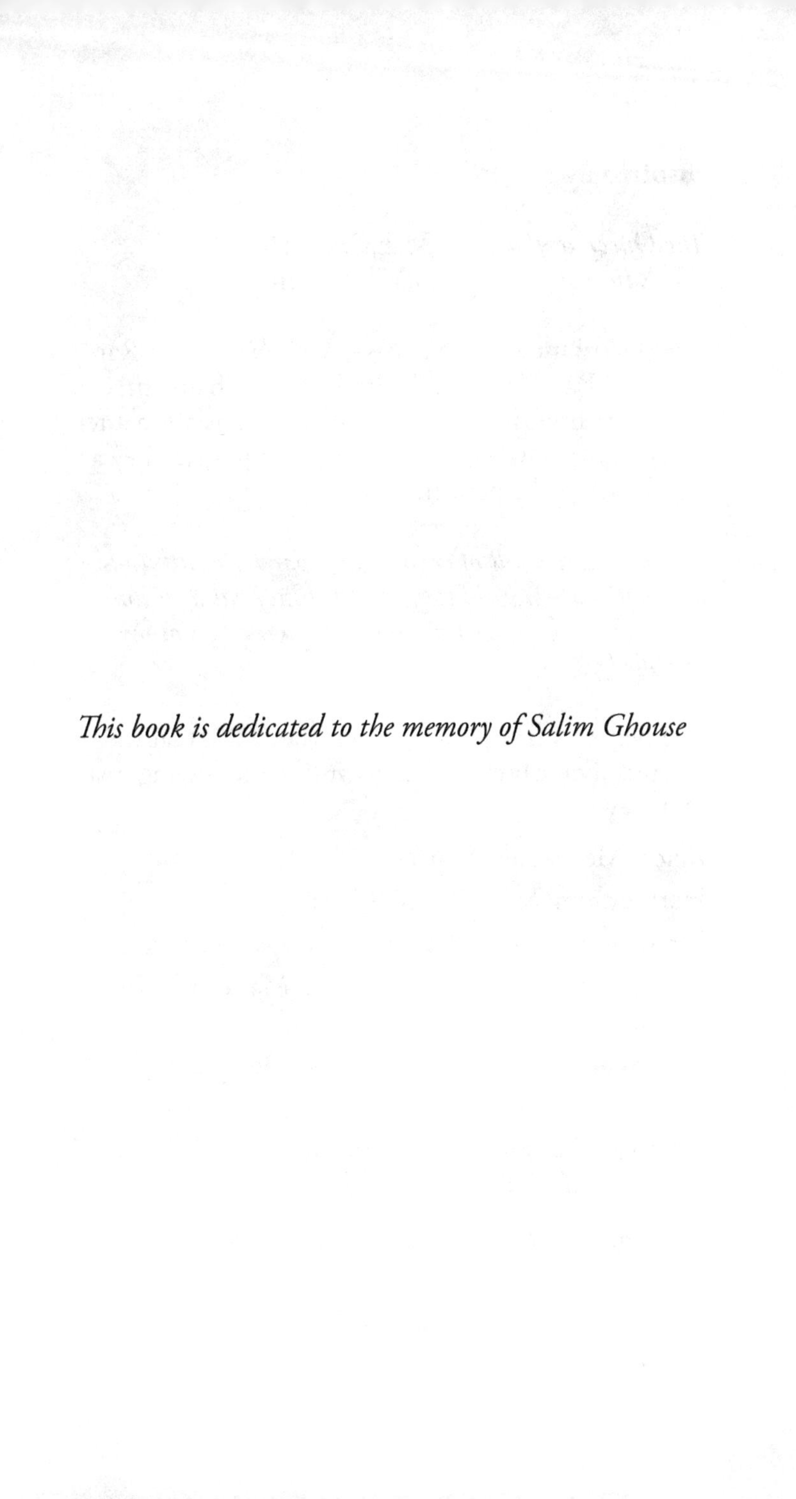

This book is dedicated to the memory of Salim Ghouse

Inspired by

The Queen of Jhansi by Mahasweta Devi
The Ranee of Jhansi by D.V.Tahamankar

The poetry used in the play—*Jhansi ki Rani* on Rani Lakshmi Bai—is by Subhadra Kumari Chauhan.* Here, the English transliteration and translation after every stanza have been provided for support. They are not a part of the performance.

This play is a result of creative and patriotic enthusiasm and not a lesson in history; albeit, historical facts and significances have been maintained to the best of my knowledge.

The play was first performed in March 2016 at the Alliance Française of Madras with the following cast and crew:

Actor: Meera Sitaraman

Harmonium: Srivaralaxmi 'Maya'

Percussion and Choreography: Vishwa Bharath

Music Composition: Srivaralaxmi 'Maya' and Nithya Sivashankar**

Design and Direction: V Balakrishnan

Photographs are from the performance at Alliance Française of Madras.

Photographs: M Sivanesan, C Vishwajith

** The entire poem is available online. The play, however, uses excerpts from it.*
***The poems in the play were sung.*

Introduction

In the Indian chapter of the Royal Court Theatre's workshop for directors and playwrights (Bangalore 2001), facilitator Ramin Gray educated us that a playwright is a person who makes plays, and not writes them (the word 'wright' being old English for a craftsperson or builder, e.g., wheelwright, cartwright). Till then, I was convinced that this seemingly tough work of creativity required astute knowledge of grammar and sentence formation. After returning from the London chapter of the RCT residency (having attended sessions by Martin Crimp, Caryl Churchill and so many other fascinating makers of plays), I decided to attempt to make a play. My endeavours slowly revealed to me that it was not unlike the process I followed as an actor to facilitate the illusion of a character in the minds of my audience. The task was bare open in its demand. I had to be intuitive in my writing—no forced flowery language, no showing off, but honest, truthful and organic writing. My first calling has always been that of an actor, the facilitator of the illusion, the magician. I became a director out of compulsion (no one was casting me), and now I wanted to make plays that I wanted to articulate on stage. History, legends and myths were my sources of nourishment, feeding my daydreams and imagination, and subsequently providing the building blocks for my plays. (Later, I did make plays like *Sordid*, *Margazhi*, *God's Will* and *Glue*, which came from my present interactions with life.)

How I responded to myths and legends became my plays. How I daydreamed about people from history became my plays. How I sought liberation through these role-plays became my plays. *Gallantly Fought the Queen* is my excitement and goosebumps transformed to words. Meera Sitaraman took training in swordplay, folk dance, and music to create the play, and has made it her own. I am satiated in the knowledge that this play has stood the test of an audience ample times before coming out as a published play. I mean, what is the purpose of a play but to be performed. If they get published as well, it's nice. For this, I would like to thank my dear friend Nandini Krishnan (a fascinating writer and maker of plays) who trusts my words and what they generate.

V Balakrishnan
October 2022

सिंहासन हिल उठे राजवंशों ने भृकुटी तानी थी
बूढ़े भारत में आई फिर से नयी जवानी थी
गुमी हुई आज़ादी की कीमत सबने पहचानी थी
दूर फिरंगी को करने की सबने मन में ठानी थी
चमक उठी सन सत्तावन में, वह तलवार पुरानी थी
कानपूर के नाना की मुँहबोली बहन छबीली थी
हुई वीरता की वैभव के साथ सगाई झाँसी में
ब्याह हुआ रानी बन आई लक्ष्मीबाई झाँसी में
उदित हुआ सौभाग्य, मुदित महलों में उजियाली छाई
किंतु कालगति चुपके-चुपके काली घटा घेर लाई
तीर चलाने वाले कर में उसे चूड़ियाँ कब भाई
रानी विधवा हुई, हाय! विधि को भी नहीं दया आई
निसंतान मरे राजाजी रानी शोक-समानी थी
बुझा दीप झाँसी का तब डलहौज़ी मन में हरषाया
राज्य हड़प करने का उसने यह अच्छा अवसर पाया
फ़ौरन फौजें भेज दुर्ग पर अपना झंडा फहराया

sinhaasan hil uthe rajvanshon ne bhrikuti taani thi
boodhe Bhaarat mein aayi phir se nayi jawaani thi
gumi hui aazaadi ki keemat sabne pehchaani thi
door phirangi ko karne ki sabne mann mein thaani thi
chamak uthi sann sattaavan mein, woh talwaar purani thi
Kanpur ke Nana ki munhboli behen Chhabeeli thi
hui veerta ki vaibhav ke saath sagaai Jhansi mein
byaah hua rani ban aayi Lakshmi Bai Jhansi mein
udit hua saubhaagya, mudit mehelon mein ujiyaali chhaayi
kintu kaalgati chupke-chupke kaali ghataa gher laayi
teer chalaane waale kar mein use choodiyan kab bhaayi
Rani vidhva hui haaye vidhi ko bhi nahin dayaa aayi
nissantaan mare Rajaji, Rani shok samaani thi

bujha deep Jhansi ka tab Dalhousie mann mein harshaaya
rajya hadap karne ka usne ye achcha avasar paayaa
phoren faujein bhej durg par apnaa jhanda phehraaya

*The royal thrones were shaken off their stupor as the dynasties
girdled themselves.
A young vigour was seen growing again in ancient India.
The worth of the freedom lost was realised by all.
To keep the British at bay was the determination of all.
The sword that glistened in 1857 had seen many battles.
Chhabeeli was the honorary sister of the Nana of Kanpur.
Valour[1] and wealth[2] were engaged in Jhansi.
With marriage, Lakshmi Bai became the Queen of Jhansi.
Good luck prospered and the old palace gained light.
However, with time, quietly, darkness engulfed it.
For one who shot arrows, bangles were never an attraction—
the Queen was widowed, sigh! Even fate was merciless.
The King died childless and left the Queen distraught.
It was when this light extinguished in Jhansi, that Dalhousie was
silently joyous.
To usurp the kingdom, he found it to be opportune, and
sent immediately his troops to hoist the Union Jack at the fort.*

---

1 Referring to Lakshmi Bai.

2 Referring to the King and his kingdom.

1

"Meri Jhansi nahi doongi."[3]

I was surprised at my own tone,
resonating with power.
I had heard whispered that I was sweet and beautiful,
but unfortunately,
had a comical shrill voice.
Now it sounded as never,
to tell Dalhousie I was not consenting
to be a pushover.

---

3 I won't part with my Jhansi.

C Vishwajith

2

I was deposed and deprived of power,
and unable to help the people
who called me "Our mother."

No more a regent to my son,
nor will he ascend the throne.
No more than a Hindu widow,
of hope and aim shorn.

3

The agent of the British, Major Ellis,
compassionate towards me,
but loyal to his masters,
told me it was all over.
What the English won, the English kept.
What was a gift had run its course.
And now I needed to go gently
or would be made to leave by force.

4

I dismissed my ministers and attendants.
Bitterly did I weep…
Did not partake food or drink,
and paced the palace's keep.

I heard my father speak to my people,
"All is not lost.
The Rani will find a way."

Brave words, Father. What way now can there be?
But I was not born to cry.

5

Major Ellis delivered the verdict of dismay and left.

Dalhousie was adamant.

I invited John Lang, an able counsel, to plead my cause.

I wanted to appeal to London.

Surely the Queen will see… A woman can

man a man's world with aplomb.

John Lang advised me

to draw the pension,

not break the calm.

But that would bias my adopted son's rights

to his father's lands.

A pensioner he was not born to be,

but a rightful heir.

I refused the demand.

छिनी राजधानी दिल्ली की, लखनऊ छीना बातों-बात
कैद पेशवा था बिठुर में, हुआ नागपुर का भी घात
उदैपुर, तंजौर, सतारा, करनाटक की कौन बिसात
जबकि सिंध, पंजाब, ब्रह्म पर अभी हुआ था वज्र-निपात
बंगाले, मद्रास आदि की भी तो वही कहानी थी

chhini rajdhani Dilli ki, Lucknow chheena baaton baat
qaid Peshwa tha Bithur mein, hua Nagpur ka bhi ghaat
Udaipur, Tanjore, Sattara, Karnatak ki kaun bisaat
jabki Sindh, Punjab, Brahm par abhi hua tha vajr nipaat
Bangale, Madras aadi ki bhi toh vahi kahaani thi

The capital, Delhi, was snatched; snatched too was
Lucknow by mere talk.
The Peshwa was imprisoned in Bithur, while Nagpur was
ambushed.
Udaipur, Tanjore, Sattara and Karnatak too were lost easily.
At the same time, Sindh, Punjab and Brahm had been struck as
if by lightning.
The same story repeated in Bengal and Madras.

6

The governor general's diktat held firm.
I lost the case.
My husband's property, jewels
and personal belongings
were to be conveyed to my son when he came of age.
He was good for inheritance,
but not for coronation.

लावारिस का वारिस बनकर ब्रिटिश राज्य झाँसी आया
अश्रुपूर्णा रानी ने देखा झाँसी हुई बिरानी थी
अनुनय विनय नहीं सुनती है, विकट शासकों की माया
व्यापारी बन दया चाहता था जब यह भारत आया
डलहौज़ी ने पैर पसारे, अब तो पलट गई काया
राजाओं नव्वाबों को भी उसने पैरों ठुकराया
रानी दासी बनी, बनी यह दासी अब महरानी थी

lawaris ka waris bankar British rajya Jhansi aaya
ashrupoorna Rani ne dekha Jhansi hui biraani thi
anunay vinay nahin sunti hai, vikat shaasakon ki maaya
vyaapaari ban dayaa chahta tha jab yeh Bhaarat aaya
Dalhousie ne pair pasaare, ab toh palat gayi kaaya
rajaon nawabon ko bhi usne pairon thukraaya
Rani daasi bani, bani yeh daasi ab Maharani thi

The British came to Jhansi like an heir to the heirless.
The tearful Queen saw the desertion of Jhansi.
The formidable rulers did not heed to persuasion or petition.
The British came seeking pity as businessmen to India.
Dalhousie spread his reach and the context upturned.
He disrespectfully rejected the Rajahs and the Nawabs.
The Queen was enslaved, and this slave became a
Maharani.

7

Three years passed in uneventful silence.
I spoke to my people freely and without reserve.
I shared in their indignities and sufferings.
I was the remainder of their disgrace
and a challenge
to their Bundelkhandi pride.

8

My city was muted and silent.
New found relations resented.
The usury and the borrower
were bonded through centuries
by salt, blood and ashes.
And now those generations old ties lay severed
by Englishmen sitting in government office.
Jhansi was swallowed in the Company's Raj.
The army at large…
Soldiers returned, disbanded, disrobed, discharged.
A burden on hard-pressed families…
destitution followed.
The sinews, muscles and pride
now hollowed.

9

The back was laden with
whiplashes and insulting blows,
and soon the greased cartridge was to follow.
Arose, arose, arose the angry bile…
and foamed out of the Indian mouth.
At first, a crack, then crackling like fire.

10

Hate for the British grew,
and I heard whispers of a revolt.
The men were not ones to be
noosed around the neck,
and the imperial yoke was stifling
the free, relentless spirit of us all.

11

Mangalam[4] denotes the end of a performance,
but in 1857 it saw the commencement.
Mangal Pandey fired,
with steady hands, the fatal shot.
Rotis and lotus petals announced their presence.
Delhi was the headquarters.
The Mughal was back
on his throne.
Hatred simmered and hissed,
but the English were blissfully unaware
of a trodden people's spirit.
And Major Skene went on record to say,
"There is no cause of alarm in this neighbourhood."
The date was May 18th, 1857.

---

4 A concluding dance piece that seeks blessings, and denotes the culmination of a performance.

12

Meerut, Delhi, Lucknow, Kanpur, Sitapur.
The flags changed colours;
the command was in the vernacular.
Benares and Allahabad rose, but fell.
Bahadur Shah Zafar, the last Mughal,
was touted to the throne.
At Meerut, Kanpur, and Orchha, the English
were burned down.

महलों ने दी आग, झोंपड़ी ने ज्वाला सुलगाई थी
यह स्वतंत्रता की चिनगारी अंतरतम से आई थी
झाँसी चेती, दिल्ली चेती, लखनऊ लपटें छाई थी
मेरठ, कानपूर, पटना ने भारी धूम मचाई थी
जबलपूर, कोल्हापूर में भी कुछ हलचल उकसानी थी

mahalon ne di aag, jhonpdi ne jwaala sulgaayi thi
yeh swatantrata ki chingari antartam se aayi thi
Jhansi cheti, Dilli cheti, Lucknow laptein chhaayi thi
Meerut, Kanpur, Patna ne bhaari dhoom machaayi thi
Jabalpur, Kolhapur mein bhi kuch hulchul uksaani thi

The palaces gave birth to fires of revolt, even huts kindled the flames.
This spark of freedom was ignited from within.

Jhansi awoke, Delhi awoke, Lucknow felt it too.
Even Meerut, Kanpur and Patna were ready to fervently revolt.
Jabalpur, Kolhapur too needed to be stirred.

13

The soldiers in Jhansi revolted.
The English in the Star Fort were condemned.
The rebellion was a fire
and its tongue licked Jhansi.
The Star Fort fell, and the
English barricaded themselves.

14

I offered to house the women and children,
and keep them safe.
The English were unimpressed.
I was a queen without a kingdom…
one who had no British allegiance.
They felt
to trust me with their families was unwise
and would result in a tragedy.
The flames that were on the rise
were not of a tameable kind… Never
has inferno been.
The floods, the fires, and rebels
would see no king, no queen.

I too would be submerged in the uprising,
but women and children
I could protect.
From my place, the foolish English
removed their families,
and the result
was disastrous.

15

The sepoys surrounded the fort.
The English fell.
The context was upturned. Three officers—
Purcell, Scott and Andrew—were killed.
The British fought and shot, and held
the fort for a short while,
but then, out of ammunition and help,
decided to the rebels, surrender.

16

The Fort of Jhansi raised a white flag.
The British filed out to supposed safety
under promise of safe passage.

Jokhan Bagh was to host a massacre.
66 Englishmen, women and children
were killed.
What happened?
Who ordered the kill?
I was unaware, but the
mutiny was to be impaired
by this act of perverse warfare.

17

I was faced with a difficult decision.
Delhi was the converging point
for every rebel,
and those at Jhansi too
decided to leave;
and that was to my relief.

But they demanded 3 lakh rupees—
a reward for freeing Jhansi.

18

I was appalled
at what took place at Jokhan Bagh…
Their blood thirst, their cruelty.
Then there was the prospect of ruling Jhansi
and the inevitable clash with the English.
What must I do?

19

I waited for a sign… Which way to go?
To support the rebels and announce my freedom
or to oppose them in hope of English redemption?
The priests confused me
with their complex readings into stars
and flowers that fell of their own accord.
Pressure was mounting…
Rivals to the throne were rising.
I yielded, and gave the rebels money.
They left, and left me Jhansi
which they had freed.

The lusty sepoys, to Delhi, decided to march.
With all my money, they did depart.

20

Now to handle the English.
I knew they would be back
and with a vengeance.
They would not take the graves
of women and children
as a price of war.
I would be held responsible,
although god knew I tried my best.
I sent my bodyguards to protect the English in the
fort.
Bread, milk and water to feed
their terrified bodies and souls.
Could bread answer for blood?
I don't think so.
I wrote to Calcutta,
an attempt at diplomacy.

21

"The troops stationed at Jhansi
were unfaithful and cruel.
They killed all the Europeans,
clerks, military and their families.
I deeply regret I could not rush to their aid
as I lacked men, guns and ammunition.
The sepoys threatened me with canons,
to blow up my house,
and extorted money and property
in exchange for my honour and life.
With no British left in Jhansi,
who will maintain
the subordinate agencies—
the police, the judiciary?
I am holding together body and soul,
but your advice is solicited—
to keep or abjure control?"

22

The massacre of Jokhan Bagh
saw me, with British permission, take charge.
In peacetime they refused to hand it to me,
and now when they could not keep it,
wanted me to bear the cross.
I was to be their agent,
keep the stables clean.

I was induced to address orders,
requesting all to stay in their posts
and render their duties to the state.
No word of thanks for my role.
Not a sign of gratitude.

Just an ungraceful proclamation
to exhibit the arrogance of entitled attitude.
I wrote back,
"I live in fear for my life and my citizens.
I have no means to provide
for the state or its safety.

I have given all I had to the rebels,
to save the massacre of my town.
But I can't in the future,
without money or competent men,
to our cause, nurture and tend."

23

I received a reply, begging me
to manage the district for the British.
Collecting taxes and raising the police
till the charge be taken over,
and I will relinquish it, and be paid
for my troubles and usances.
While the Britishers' faith in me
was compelling,
it was sheer bureaucratic diplomacy
and nothing more.

It was clear… once the storm abated,
I would not be commemorated,
but would have to answer to a British court
for my role in the Jhansi episode.
I was to be tried as a party
to the rebels' actions at Jokhan Bagh.
They were biding their time,
before they could descend on me
and send me to perdition.

24

With the British at bay for the time,
my people had to be cheered and comforted.
I spoke to them to hold courage
till all was sorted,
"With great difficulty we were able
to save the city from being looted
by the frenzied sepoys.
They have gone away
and I hope for good,
but they have left behind chaos and disarray
which we must put right without delay.
At any rate, we must see
that the citizens of Jhansi
are not harassed and molested,
that anarchy does not raise its head.
The British want me to be in charge
until everything returns to right,
and then they will rule you again.
I call upon you, my citizens,
to advise me with your experience.
Please speak your minds
freely and frankly."

25

The people wanted my rule—
a free and independent Jhansi—
not the British to return
and take over their country.
And so it was to be.
I was a queen once more.
"Maintain order, punctuality, firmness and vigilance,
and do your duty."
Work and more work was our motto.

But what I feared was soon cemented.
My spies in Fort William, Calcutta,
informed me that it was all a ruse.
A matter of months.
And once the revolt was quelled
and peace was restored,
I was to be tried for murder.
I had been prejudged and sentenced
without a chance to speak my side.
And I decided to fight for my honour.

26

To be called a rebel,
even worse, Jezebel
I could manage.
But to be accused of being a murderer…
That I could not tolerate.
Anger and indignation were fine,
but Jhansi's strength on the battlefield
could never compare to that of the British.
To face them, to fight without preparations,
was imprudent and stupid.

I decided to play the waiting game.
There was time before the English arrived.
It was not to be today or tomorrow
but that they would was sure.
And I wanted to be equipped and prepared,
to let them know Jhansi was not going to be
a walkover.
It would be death or the fame of the earth—
in this or another birth.

C Vishwajith

हतो वा प्राप्स्यसि स्वर्गं जित्वा वा भोक्ष्यसे महीम् |
तस्मादुत्तिष्ठ कौन्तेय युद्धाय कृतनिश्चयः || 37 ||

hato vaa praapsyasi swargam jitvaa vaa bhokshyase mahim
tasmaad utthistha kaunteya yuddhaaya krita-nischayah[5]

Slain, you will obtain heaven; victorious, you will enjoy the earth; therefore, stand up, O son of Kunti, determined to fight.

---

5 Bhagavad Gita: Chapter 2, Verse 37.

27

The task before me was not a light one,
nor was I experienced.
I wanted vision, energy and determination.
As I was wandering in this *chakravyuha*[6],
I faced my first battle.

6 An impenetrable battle array (used as a metaphorical reference here).

28

Sadasheo Rau, my dead husband's nephew,
made himself a throne and sat on it,
and called it Jhansi.
I had him arrested.
Hardly a skirmish.
But more was to come.

29

The Orchha Rani,
Larhi Bai, the warrior amazon,
sent her troops.
Nathay Khan was her ace of swords.
A magnificent general,
but a bad politician.
He promised to give me a pension
if I surrendered.
I promised him better,
"Do your best. I will make you a woman
like the one you serve,
or better, like the one you fight."

30

The army of Nathay Khan was approaching.
My army assembled,
and I had an eye for the spectacular.
I tied orange thread of silk
on the wrists of the men;
commanded them with the army.
The Khan rode into my trap.
I did not oppose him for a lengthy while…
Lengthy, just enough for him
to come into the range of my guns
and then they spoke fire.
Khuda Baksh was my gunner;
Kadak Bijli, my favourite cannon.
And together, they celebrated Diwali early.

उत रिपुदल सेना उमड़ आइ। चहुं ओर मनो घन घटा छाइ।
बरछिन की माल चमंक रही। सोउ दामिन मनौ दमंक रही।
जहं तहं तोपन को होत सोर। सोई मानों हो रई घटा घोर।
गज खच्चर बाज चिकारत हैं। पिक कोकिल मोर अलापत हैं।
उठ धुंआ गुंग नभ लेत गहे। मानों धुर चौगृद टूट रहे।
सबकी बातन कौ मची सोर। है मनो पवन कौ जोर तो।

ut ripudal sena umad aayi | chahoon ore mano ghan ghataa
chhaayi |
barchhin ki maal chamank rahi | saudaamin manau damank
rahi |
jahan tahan topan ko hot sor | soi maano ho rai ghataa ghor |
gaj kachchar baaj chikaarat hain | pik kokil mor alaapat hain |
uth dhuan gung nabh let gaye | maano dhur chaugrit toot
rahe |
sabki baatan kau machau sor | hai mano pavan kau jor toh |

The enemies gathered like dark clouds on all four sides.
The spears shone, like lightning they flashed.
The sound of the canons roared like clouds clashing with each
other.
Elephants, horses and eagles were alert while the birds of peace
were missing.
The rising smoke covered the skies like it was shattering to
pieces.
The war cries raised a ruckus and blew like strong winds.

Nathay Khan lost,

and my sister queen sued for peace.

But men have such egos. Nathay Khan

rushed to the British

and spoke of me being in league with the rebels.

The scales in Calcutta tipped.

The British had what they were waiting for—

another piece of unrequited evidence;
another opportunity to seize Jhansi.
And I was two battles old.

31

One year of peace.
Elsewhere in India, the rebels
were losing again and again.
The British were organized and centrally directed.
The rebels were with cause,
but not coordination.
We were small states and towns,
they were a nation.
If the British had lost, even then,
Jhansi would have to fight Delhi.

My duty to Jhansi was my duty to India.
We had achieved our war aim. Jhansi was free.
No, I did not send help to the rebels.
Jhansi needed peace and tranquility.

32

The emperor, the blood of Genghis Khan and Babur,
was arrested.
His sons shot… so much
for trusting the British honour.
The rebellion lost its centre.
Defeat came gradually but with certainty.
Nana Saheb lost in Kanpur.
They lost their *Peshwai*[7] at Bithur.
The embers of revolt were quelled in Awadh.

---

7 The Peshwa's land (ownership). The Peshwa was the appointed prime minister of the Maratha Empire.

33

And Gwalior… Gwalior was the cleanest sword.
That which never left its sheath.
Scindia did not strike against the British.
Scindia did not join the rebellion.
Scindia should have thrown his lot with the rebels;
then, the fight would have been national, not local;
then, the fight would have been between India and
England,
not presidencies versus the Empire.
Every warrior in the north and south would have
gathered
and would have left no scope for speculation.
The British would be out,
and this the British knew.
But Scindia, Scindia did not strike.

इस स्वतंत्रता महायज्ञ में कई वीरवर आए काम
नाना धुंधूपंत, ताँतिया, चतुर अज़ीमुल्ला सरनाम
अहमदशाह मौलवी, ठाकुर कुँवरसिंह सैनिक अभिराम
भारत के इतिहास गगन में अमर रहेंगे जिनके नाम

is swatantrata mahaayagya mein kayi veervar aaye kaam
Nana Dhundhopant, Tantia, chatur Azimullah sarnaam
Ahmadshah Maulvi, Thakur Kunwar Singh sainik abhiraam
Bhaarat ke itihaas gagan mein amar rahenge jinke naam

In this great sacrifice for freedom, several warriors laid their lives.
Nana Dhundhopant, Tatya, and the clever Azimullah,
Ahmadshah Maulvi, Thakur Kunwar Singh with their entire
military.
In the historic skies of India, their names will remain immortal.

34

Delhi recaptured. Awadh ruptured.
Only Jhansi remained to be destroyed.
War was inevitable,
but I made one more attempt to buy peace—another
letter to the masters.
It failed.

35

To be arrested
and tried in a court with known consequences
or to go to war
with courageous significances?
What must I do?
Suffer alone in prison or
the executioner's block?
Or make oblations of all my people to the British
sword?
What is my Dharma?
To my soil, to my people, to myself?
One measly life; one Lakshmi Bai dead
and all my people safe…
Or all of us dead,
never to return nor again be brave?
To go forward was dangerous,
but to go back was impossible.
I decided to fight—to fight to the finish.

सर्वधर्मान्परित्यज्य मामेकं शरणं व्रज |
अहं त्वां सर्वपापेभ्यो मोक्षयिष्यामि मा शुचः || 66 ||

sarva-dharmaan parityajya maam ekam sharanam vraja
aham tvaam sarva-paapebhyo mokshayishyaami maa shuchah[8]

*Abandoning all dharmas, (of the body, mind, and intellect), take
refuge in Me alone; I will liberate thee from all sins; grieve not.*

---

8 Bhagavad Gita: Chapter 18, Verse 66.

36

We unearthed our cannons
and joyously unearthed men and women too.
The amazons of Jhansi
could fence, ride and shoot
just as well as our men could.
The discouraged and cowardly
made a beeline for Gwalior,
for there, there was no trouble to be expected.
Gwalior was the Britishers' best friend.
But what if this became a trend?
Jhansi would be empty.
Something was needed to show
that I was not suicidal in my decisions.
My war assumptions
held potential of life.

I decided to hold the ceremony
of *haldi-kumkum*[9] adornment.
Every woman in the city decked and jewelled;

---

9 Turmeric powder used for social and religious markings.

every man, dressed to kill. Literally.
I leaned back in my white sari,
to see my people so happy
in spite of what was possibly
now beyond auguries and prophecy.

37

No half measures from my enemies.
It was to be a formidable adversary.
I would have to face in battle
the tested and scarred fox of Egypt,
of Malta, and Ireland.
Born in Germany…
thrice awarded for gallantry…
the hero of Syria…
Sir Hugh Rose
was marching against me.

38

I was thirty years old,
without any experience of modern warfare.
He had British and Indian troops,
sappers and miners, a siege train,
infantry, cavalry, and artillery of various calibres.
An impressive array.
I almost felt enthralled
at such a glowing tribute.

39

Sir Hugh rested his troops and then moved.
Sehore and Rahatgarh fell.
The Rohilas and Afghans fought well.
Next to be captured was Baroda.
Sagar was a willing ally.
The roads to the north and west lay open now.
Garhakota was the first eastern obstacle to be
conquered.
Now the road to Jhansi was cleared.

40

Inch by inch Sir Hugh rolled on.
The Bundelas would not concede their territory
without a fight, not so easily.
But even their resolve could not
postpone the inevitable.
Soon, Jhansi was in the English gunner's sight.

41

I appealed to my childhood friends—
Rao Sahib and Tatya Tope to come to my help.
I was under no illusions
to what my fate would be
if I was captured alive,
but my people, they had a right to decide
what their fate should be.
I asked my ministers, chiefs and citizens,
"Should we sue for peace or defend the city?"
What followed was din and shouting…
It took me a while to understand.
The verdict was unanimous—war.
We fight for independence.

वीर सैनिकों के मन में था अपने पुरखों का अभिमान
नाना धुंधूपंत पेशवा जुटा रहा था सब सामान
बहिन छबीली ने रण-चण्डी का कर दिया प्रकट आह्वान
हुआ यज्ञ प्रारम्भ उन्हें तो सोई ज्योति जगानी थी

veer sainikon ke mann mein tha apne purkhon ka abhimaan
Nana Dhundhopant Peshwa juta raha tha sab saamaan
behen Chhabeeli ne Rann-chandi ka kar diya prakat aahvaan
hua yagya praarambh unhe toh soyi jyoti jagaani thi

64

The heroic soldiers bore the pride of their ancestors in their hearts.
Nana Dhundhopant, the Peshwa, was gathering all the war
materials.
His sister Chhabeeli invoked the goddess Rann-chandi within her.
The sacrifice started, as they incited the extinguished flames.

42

The walls were repaired and strengthened,
men and women enlisted,
the bastions and turrets were manned night and day.
The coming storm was daunting.
The battle for Jhansi started.
25th March, the English guns
began to bombard the city.
Never-ending fire, relentlessly.
We answered shot for shot.
On the evening of the 31st,
at a distance,
was spotted hope. It was the Peshwa's regiment.

43

Tatya Tope, with the Peshwa's army,
was coming to help Jhansi.
Tatya lit an immense bonfire.
I answered by firing torrents from all the cannons.
We, the besieged, were sighting liberation.

44

Sir Hugh decided to meet his enemy
in a head-on collision.
He had lesser men
but smarter strategies.
It was a gamble, but a gamble he had to take.
Tatya attacked.

तात्या टोपे चालकरणी हल्ला
करण्या आला आ sss[10] |
ऐकूनी झाला शत्रु घाबरला |
वंदन करितो आम्ही त्याला रे जी sss |
वंदना करितो आम्ही त्याला रे जी sss |

Tatya Tope chaalkarni halla karnya aalaa |
aikuni jhaala shatru ghaabarlaa |
vandana karitoh aahmi tyaala re ji |
vandana karitoh aahmi tyaala re ji |

Tatya Tope strategized to attack fiercely.
Hearing this, the enemy got scared.
We salute him!
We salute him!

---

10 This is a traditional Marathi ballad that falls under the genre called
'Powada'. The SSS after the lines denote repetition of the last word to
the beat of the music. In this case, 6 times.

Extraordinarily, Tatya lost.
What was a game of chess,
Tatya mistook to be boys throwing mud balls.
He lost guns, and many materials of war,
he lost his place in history,
and he lost Jhansi.
20,000 men defeated
by 1500 Englishmen…
Tatya's faulty tactics.
Jhansi was seeped in gloom,
humiliation and bitterness.
Jubilation turned into depression.
I was silenced,
but despair is an unworthy companion.
The enemy had to be quelled.
The people had to be fed
patriotic ardour and truth.

45

"For the last ten days,
Jhansi has been putting up a heroic fight
without the Peshwa's help.
We have seen the plight of their army,
but it does not matter.
We will not lose heart, we will fight to the last.
You have fought with matchless courage
and determination,
you have endured and suffered.
Now, we will be fighting the final battle,
and I rely upon you
to maintain the highest standards of heroism
and discipline.
We will defend Jhansi
to the last man.
I know you will do it.
Har Har Mahadev.[11]"

---

11 A war cry praising Lord Shiva.

C Vishwajith

46

Red hot balls from the cannons fell, fell, fell…
I girdled my sword and went.
The silenced guns were reopened.
The palace was the target. Glass shattered.
One by one the rooms were shelled.
Traitor Dulaji Thakur opened the gates
for the Englishmen.
Ladders were hoisted
and the English climbed the fort.
Storm of bullets… rockets formed a sheet of fire.
The English were stubborn and resisted.
Death was now a drunken dancer let loose.
I was on the scene; I used my binoculars
to sight hundreds of men
carrying bundles of grass.
They made steps for the English to climb on
and besiege the ramparts.
My soldiers were being cut to pieces.
I was pale, speechless…
Then I was myself again…

I led my 1500 Arab and Afghan regulars into the fray.
Hand to hand,
sword on sword,
men rolled in the dust.
The British ran.
Death was flying with mercurial speed.
The English were silent as death.
Citizens and soldiers
fought shoulder to shoulder.
1500 became 40.
The English guns were very thirsty…
All the blood they spilled
and screamed again for a refill.

47

My forty Afghan guards
fought 150 Englishmen;
first with guns and then swords.
The British, for amusement, set them on fire.
They were half-burnt, their clothes in flames;
they rushed out, hacking at their assailants
with swords in both hands, till they were shot,
bayoneted… struggling, even while dying
on the ground, to strike again.

48

Who were you, my brothers?
What was your resolve?
That you died protecting my honour…
We were not one by blood,
we were not one by religion.
But like hawks on vulgar pigeons,
you made them shiver in fear.
What was your decision?
To fight alongside your sister?
For we partook of the same air and elements;
we ate the grains of the same fields,
and your laughter
must have mingled with mine…
No different was my war cry from yours.
Mahadev[12] will steal away grief,
and Allah is great…
And so are you today, my Afghan brothers.
You elated me with your blood,
and your greatness in heaven will see

---

12 Lord Shiva.

the rewards of a million gods,
or one… if that the truth be.
Till we meet again,
blood will be answered with blood.

49

In disarray, beyond plans and designs,
I slashed and cut,
shot and felled;
I was blind with rage.
My Jhansi was falling.
I was bodily removed from the fray;
to my palace was taken away.
I had checked, not dislodged.
I wanted to hunt down the enemy.
I rushed dagger in hand…

My seventy-five year old chief
stopped me, held me back and said,
"To be killed by their bullets
is as useless
as dying an ignoble death."

50

I was in the palace crying bitterly.
I did not know what would happen to me, to my city.

"I have made up my mind not to surrender,
but to blow myself up with gunpowder.
Those of you who want to follow
and die with me, remain. The rest,
leave the fort when it is dark.
Jai Bhavani[13]… Har Har Mahadev."

My chief scolded me
for having suggested suicide.
The battle was not the war…
where was my pride?
Another suggestion was made—
to leave the city by stealth
and make for the Peshwa's camp.
To live, to fight another day.
I touched his feet as a daughter should do.
His wisdom saved me
from what I was about to do.

---

13 A war cry praising Goddess Bhavani.

51

Men were put to death.
Children and women, burnt.
The palace was plundered,
homes desecrated.
The soldiers waited impatiently while their masters
played the looting game.
Then it was the turn of the Indian sepoys,
and Hugh Rose ordered
an indiscriminate slaughter of people.

रानी रोयीं रिनवासों में, बेगम ग़ाम से थीं बेज़ार
उनके गहने कपड़े बिकते थे कलकत्ते के बाज़ार
सरे आम नीलाम छापते थे अंग्रेज़ों के अखबार
'नागपूर के ज़ेवर ले लो लखनऊ के लो नौलख हार'
यों परदे की इज़्ज़त परदेशी के हाथ बिकानी थी

Rani royin rinvaason mein, begum gum se thi bezaar
unke gehne kapde bikte the Kalkatte ke bazaar
sare aam nilaam chhaapte the angrezon ke akhbaar
'Nagpur ke zevar le lo, Lucknow ke lo naulakha haar'
yon parde ki izzat pardeshi ke haath bikaani thi

The Queen wept in her palace, and was bereft with grief.
Her jewellery, clothes were being sold in the markets of Calcutta.

The English newspapers openly printed the auction:
'Buy the jewels of Nagpur, buy the expensive necklace of
Lucknow.'
Thus, the honour of the veil was sold at the hands of the British.

52

One last look at my city.
One final salute to history.
One eyeful of sustenance for the days to roll by.
That day was familiar,
as if it had been courted by history
for eons and ages;
as if time knew what the day would look like
and prepared it like a bride…
for centuries of stories held the city of Jhansi.
Virsingha had built it to contend
with lions and elephants,
but jackals had brought it down.
His cataract eyes
only saw a mist, a veil, a Jhansi.
To me, the fires were as clear as my conscious.
Nothing was hidden from my sight.
On the cobblestone paths
and alleys between the closely packed houses,
young boys, Pathans, Afghans, Bundelas and Marathas
had fought to the end

on grounds slippery with blood.

I saw Jhansi in flames.

Jhansi was ravaged, raped, and ruined.

My men, women and books, burnt.

My city and its wealth, auctioned.

How clear was the sky

when death tiptoed, to befell.

The last standing to dispel.

The gloom and dismay of death's knell.

Debts to the motherland were being cleared

faster than accounts could be noted.

What happens once the victors

gaze on the vanquished's wealth?

Let's not discuss.

Enough to say…

Fire, blood, ashes;

burn, kill, hang;

no rituals, no rites, no obsequies;

corpses everywhere.

53

I wore my armour,

carried my dagger,

loaded my revolver,

and left on my white horse.

I was not carrying any money,

only my son Damodhar

strapped to my back.

We left the fort and were attacked by alert sentinels.

Many were killed,

many got separated.

My father was captured

and hanged.

I covered 102 miles in 24 hours on horseback,

and after a few desperate fights,

reached the camp of

Rao Saheb Peshwa.

रानी बढ़ी कालपी आई, कर सौ मील निरंतर पार
घोड़ा थक कर गिरा भूमि पर गया स्वर्ग तत्काल सिधार
यमुना तट पर अंग्रेज़ों ने फिर खाई रानी से हार

Rani badi kaalpi aayi, kar sau meel nirantar paar
ghoda thak kar gira bhoomi par gayaa swarg tatkaal sidhaar
Yamuna tat par angrezon ne phir khaayi Rani se haar

The Queen came to Kalpi, after covering 100 miles relentlessly.
The horse fell to the ground tired, and departed to the heavens.
At the Queen's hands, on the banks of the Yamuna, the English
faced defeat again.

M Sivanesan

54

I unsheathed my sword
and placed it at the Peshwa's feet.
It was the ignoble failure of his army, his commander,
that I was a fugitive.

"Your highness's illustrious forebearers
presented this weapon to us,
and with their powerful help, we used it
to do what was just and proper.
But now, we cannot have your support.
I beg to return it to you."

The Peshwa knew I had defended Jhansi.
He knew my military skill.
He gave me back my sword
and took my support.
I swore,
"Nothing will give me greater happiness
than die serving the Maratha standard
on the battlefield.
Give me men,
and I will go and fight."

55

But men will be men.
Rao Sahib was haughty;
Banda Nawab, vainglorious.
Tatya fancied himself as knowing all.
They started to begrudge me.
Perhaps they thought it was degrading
to serve under a woman.
All they had to do was lift their heads and see
the Union Jack so breezy;
the standard of a woman king.
Empress Victoria owned half the world
and these deposed kings in dusty camps
suffered from inferiority complexes.

56

Tatya was appointed the commander.
Hugh Rose was coming to Kalpi.
I knew the enemy's plans, his tactics and methods.
I drew up a strategy…
it was rejected.
What would a woman know about war?
Hugh Rose outsmarted us again.
The army of the Peshwa was sand
before the northern wind.
Tatya once again to the woods retreated, ran away.
The battle was lost,
we were on the back foot again.

57

I voted for a last-ditch fight.
"It is becoming difficult to remove ourselves
from this risky situation.
Our honour can still be retained
if we offer determined resistance.
We can win.
We have the Banda Nawab and his cannons.
They are fresh and excited to fire.
Swear to me, to fight to death.
We will win or perish
but not leave the field."

58

The men took solace and
became envigored.
Rao Sahib took the command… another mistake.
For, command is to serve,
not to abandon the cause.
He exposed his men to the enemy's fire.
They lost heart and fled.
Shots, shrapnel and shell
are powerful advocators of retreat.
I urged the Peshwa to stay and fight.
I fell upon the enemy's right-wing,
the Peshwa's left batteries opened fire.
I was twenty feet from the enemies' guns,
and would have silenced them,
when Hugh Rose entered.
With his camel forces, he advanced.
The Peshwa's men could not withstand…
collapsed our stand, our victory, our men.
And to Kalpi we had to return.
Before the sweat on our sword handles had dried,

we heard Kalpi was to be destroyed.
And we decided to evacuate. And fled.
In a familiar exercise,
the Union Jack was raised
on the final bastion of Peshwa pride.

59

We went to Gopalpur.
Tatya and the Nawab of Banda joined us.
We had lost our position, were down and discouraged.
No big guns, no horse artillery and
well-stocked magazine of ammunition.
The choice was simple before us:
be captured and hang
or live as miserable fugitives.

I could not bear to see the Maratha pride so downcast.
I don't know when the responsibility
of empowering them fell on me.
"Let us remember
that all through history,
the Maratha kings won
because of their impregnable fortresses.
What was true then, is true now.
We have lost Jhansi and Kalpi…
The enemy will soon destroy us.
We must capture a strong fort

to carry on the struggle for victory.
I think we should march on to Gwalior."

Desperate situations call for desperate measures.
I was urged by hatred, by a desire of vengeance,
by a bloodstained conscience,
by a determination to strike hard.
I recognized the possibilities before me—
Gwalior.

60

Built on a rock
impossible to ascend;
discontent and insurgent;
protected by massive walls,
Gwalior was waiting to revolt
against the Scindia and the English.
Tatya was more a Chanakya than a Chandragupta.
Tatya penetrated the city
and sowed dissent in the men;
cajoled them to join the Peshwa banner.
Scindia, at first, thought our challenge to be a bluff
and took the battlefield with his cannons.
With 200 cavalry men I charged.
Scindia's men melted.
Some left the field,
some mixed with our men;
many went to eat watermelons
in the bed of the Morar River.
Scindia ran, ran fast to join his English friends.

विजयी रानी आगे चल दी, किया ग्वालियर पर अधिकार
अंग्रेज़ों के मित्र सिंधिया ने छोड़ी रजधानी थी

vijayi Rani aage chal di, kiyaa Gwalior par adhikaar
angrezon ke mitr Scindia ne chhodi rajdhani thi

The victorious Queen surged ahead, and conquered Gwalior.
The friend of the British, Scindia, fled the capital.

61

Rao Sahib entered the city in triumph.
The palace was occupied.
The Peshwa ascended the throne.
The guns boomed 101 times…
What a waste of ammunition.
Peshwa-shahi[14] was announced:
Nana Sahib was to be Peshwa,
and Rao Sahib—the representative,
Tatya Tope—the general,
Ramrao Govind—the prime minister.
All was impressive and possibly very necessary.
The Peshwa was the new rallying point.
Some dreams he harboured…
"The Marathas in the Deccan will rise
and will unite in a common cause."
He assumed the instrument of power
but forgot he needed to wield it too.
He forgot me too.
No invitations to these festivities. I stood on my

---

14 The rule of the Peshwa.

balcony…
fireworks and smell of ghee.
Is this why thousands died at Jhansi?

62

I was impatient and worried.
The men with their feigned security
had to be rattled to reality.
I told the Peshwa
that a resounding victory over the enemy
will cement his Peshwai,
not feeding the brahmins and hosting gala festivities.
I did not see with him eye to eye,
but I could not oppose him very openly.
But I made sure he knew
I was unimpressed.

"Peshwa, the time is to make cannon balls,
not sugar balls to feed the priests.
The victory over Scindia
has gone to your head.
You feel you are the master of this land
and that is a harmful attitude.
You underrate the strength and resources of those
who made us run abandoning our forts.

They are shrewd and skillful.
Gwalior fort can fall
and it will too.
The army will desert you
if you do not enlist them in a cause.
You have the army and the treasury…
Prepare for the coming struggle.
Get the city's battlements in order;
pay the soldiers liberally,
give them able commanders.
Peshwa, this is my guidance,
and if you please, my warning."

The Peshwa did not listen to me, of course.
I was a woman ranting away.
And while he partied and played the generous host,
at the gates of the Gwalior fort,
stood Hugh Rose.

63

Tatya had the audacity to ask me for advice.
When the horses had bolted,
he wanted to close the stable doors.
"The English are getting closer…
We need to unite now
and we need your help."
I wanted to scream *I told you so.*

"When you should have been preparing for war,
you were absorbed in victory celebrations.
What can I say…
I am just an ordinary woman."
Tatya placed his turban at my feet.
I continued,
"Rao Sahib has destroyed all hopes of victory.
He ignored my warning deliberately.
He neglected the war preparations,
giving his attention to trivialities.
The enemy is upon us
and we, Tatya, are not ready.

I see nothing
but disorder and chaos.
How can we win this battle?
But I will not lose heart…
and is your heart strong too?
One glorious charge on the English.
Results, we won't care about… what do you say?
A sudden and determined attack,
and overwhelming too.
The enemy must be rolled back into hell.
I will defend the east,
we will meet on the other side.
Jaya Vijayee Bhava[15]*.* "

Tatya's gaze, his trademark smile,
I knew what he meant.
It was now to the end.
I smiled and braved myself.

नैनं छिन्दन्ति शस्त्राणि नैनं दहति पावकः |
न चैनं क्लेदयन्त्यापो न शोषयति मारुतः || 23 ||

———————————

15 May you be victorious.

nainam chhindanti shastraani nainam dahati paavakah
na chainam kledayantyaapo na shoshayati maarutah[16]

Weapons cleave it not, fire burns it not, water moistens it not, wind dries it not.

---

16 Bhagavad Gita: Chapter 2, Verse 23.

64

I gathered my men, strapped my armour.
"Bring my *shamsheer*[17] here
and my blue *chanderi*[18] *muretha*[19]."
I was in charge of 10,000 men
from the 13th of June to the 17th.
I hardly rested.
On the 17th of June,
I felt a gentle breeze,
a harbinger maybe,
of freedom and deliverance.
The blue muretha was exchanged for other colours—
the Gwalior red.
The infantry fell into battle order.
I gave the order to fire.
We advanced, covered by heavy artillery fervour.
We had determination,
we had skill,
we did not slacken or budge,
we harboured iron will.

---

17 Sword.

18 A type of silk.

19 Turban cloth.

65

Cannon fire,
gunshots,
and the smell of steel,
were regular occurrences
in my everyday life.
They were not going to frighten me,
not even cause me to pause
and think of a different strategy.
We intimidated the enemy,
we beat them back,
we had them on the run,
we made them burn
in the sun and from our guns.
The British feared the worst.

(The actor performs a martial choreography. In the performances of the play so far, the actor has been using Devarattam, a folk dance.)

66

It was 3pm.
The sun blazed
but we were winning.
The ferocious heat
was hard on the British.
'Har Har Mahadev' were the loudest shouts in the sky.
The final crisis was upon the English.

विजय मिली, पर अंग्रेज़ों की फिर सेना घिर आई थी
अबके जनरल स्मिथ सम्मुख था, उसने मुँह की खाई थी
काना और मंदरा सखियाँ रानी के संग आई थी
युद्ध क्षेत्र में उन दोनों ने भारी मार मचाई थी
पर पीछे ह्यूरोज़ आ गया, हाय! घिरी अब रानी थी

vijay mili, par angrezon ki phir sena ghir aayi thi
abke General Smith sammukh tha, usne moonh ki khaayi thi
Kaana aur Mandra sakhiyan Rani ke sang aayi thi
yudh kshetra mein un dono ne bhaari maar machaayi thi
par peechhe Hugh Rose aa gaya, haay giri ab Rani thi

*Though victory was in sight, the British army surrounded them
again.*
*Now General Smith was facing them, who had been terribly
defeated.*
Kaana and Mandra, friends of the Queen, had come with her to

the battlefield.
The two of them had wreaked havoc,
but Hugh Rose came from behind. Alas! fell the Queen.

Then the 8th hussars entered the fray,

an unanticipated contingent

we had not accounted for.

These were hardcore corps—

a contingent of well-rested, fresh soldiers,

kept hidden from the main fray,

well-fed and hydrated.

And we were tired, bloodied, bruised and thirsty.

And a massacre followed.

We were cut like vegetables.

Chaos and confusion followed.

Our cannons were seized.

I tried to form a wall of resistance

with a few dozen soldiers.

I saw my companion Mandra

shot in the chest.

The cavalry fell upon us.

I saw a man riding towards me,

he seemed to have recognized me.

I heard his screaming voice,
"He seems to be the leader,
kill him,
kill that young man."
Young man?
I laughed at his ignorance and clashed steel.
We held our ground and fought without a thought.
Killing the enemy,
slash, slash, cut, thrust.
Two swords I wielded;
the horse's reins in my mouth.
Then I felt a sword strike my forehead.
I tore my turban and arrested the flow of blood.

तो भी रानी मार काट कर चलती बनी सैन्य के पार
किन्तु सामने नाला आया, था वह संकट विषम अपार
घोड़ा अड़ा, नया घोड़ा था, इतने में आ गये अवार
रानी एक, शत्रु बहुतेरे, होने लगे वार-पर-वार
घायल होकर गिरी सिंहनी उसे वीर गति पानी थी

toh bhi Rani maar kaat kar chalti bani sainya ke paar
kintu saamne naala aaya, tha voh sankat visham apaar
ghoda ada, nayaa ghoda tha, itne mein aa gaye avaar
Rani ek, shatru bahutere, hone lage vaar par vaar
ghaayal hokar giri sinhni, use veer gati paani thi

Even then, the Queen continued to fight and move ahead.
However, a canal came ahead, an unsurmountable crisis.
The horse halted as it was a new horse, by which time the enemies arrived.
The Queen was alone, the enemies multiple, and a fierce battle ensued.
Wounded, she fell like a lioness; to achieve the glory of the brave.

67

We were outnumbered horribly
and enmeshed in the trap.
Orders in Hindi and English flew thick and fast.
In extreme danger, I decided to regroup afar.
In front of me was Sonarekha—
a small rivulet.
I decided to cross it…
When I was shot…
a carbine shot. I felt a slash.
I saw my companions horrified.
I saw my father smiling,
my husband rejoicing,
Jhalkari with her bright black eyes,
Ananda was saying he will not be scared.
I saw the people of Jhansi with haldi and kumkum,
and there was *gulal* [20] too.
They threw it in the air.
The sun was coloured…

---

20 Coloured powder used for the Indian festival of Holi.

It was dancing as if with *bhang* [21],
with red, and yellow and orange.
The colour particles hung in the air
and then fell.
And then it was all saffron,
like the Peshwa's banner.
And I was laughing and playing at his knees.
He was pulling my nose, he was joking with me,
calling me, "Chhabeeli."
The priests were smiling and speaking fast in Sanskrit.

Manikarnika naama iyam kanya
Lakshmi bhavatu
Tvam Lakshmi Bai bhava [22]

Khuda Baksh was firing Kadak Bijli.
The cannon shots were louder and louder.
My Afghan bodyguards started to dance
and were eating *laddus* [23] from the Peshwa's hands.

---

21 An edible mixture made from the buds, leaves, and flowers of marijuana.

22 May this maiden, named Manikarnika, from today, become
Lakshmi. May you be called Lakshmi Bai.

23 Indian sweet.

And then I was shouting at Major Ellis,
"Meri Jhansi nahi doongi."

And then… I don't remember.

(Light fades out on actor.)

*(Light fades in on actor to reveal them singing the poetry
and speaking the last two lines.)*

रानी गई सिधार चिता अब उसकी दिव्य सवारी थी
मिला तेज से तेज, तेज की वह सच्ची अधिकारी थी
अभी उम्र कुल तेइस की थी, मनुज नहीं अवतारी थी
हमको जीवित करने आयी बन स्वतंत्रता-नारी थी
बुंदेले हरबोलों के मुँह हमने सुनी कहानी थी
खूब लड़ी मर्दानी वह तो झाँसी वाली रानी थी

Rani gayi sidhaar, chita ab uski divya sawaari thi
mila tej se tej, tej ki voh sachchi adhikaari thi
abhi umr kul teis ki thi, manuj nahi avtaari thi
humko jeevit karne aayi, ban swatantrata naari thi
bundele harbolon ke moonh humne suni kahaani thi
khoob ladi mardaani voh toh Jhansi wali Rani thi

Rani died a martyr, the pyre was her divine chariot.
Light met light, and she was the rightful beholder of light.
She was only 23 years old [24]; a goddess, not human.

---

24 There are disparities in accounts that mention the age at which the
Rani died. The poem suggests 23, whereas folklore mention 30.

To awaken us, she became a fighter for freedom.
From the wandering minstrels of Bundela we have heard this
story—
that gallantly fought the mighty Queen of Jhansi.

रानी मर गई न होनी
अभी तो जिंदा हाउ

Rani mar gayi na honi
Abhi toh zinda hau

The Queen is not dead,
but lives on.

About the Playwright

V Balakrishnan, an alumnus of Shri Ram Centre for Performing Arts (New Delhi) and the National School of Drama (New Delhi), is the founder and artistic director of Theatre Nisha. He has directed over 210 plays, acted in over 160 plays and written more than 15 scripts.

He was awarded the Charles Wallace Scholarship to attend an International Residency with the Royal Court Theatre, London. In 2017, he was awarded the Fulbright Distinguished Award in Teaching (FDAT). In 2018, the Rotary Club of Madras East conferred the Dronacharya Award on him for his contributions to theatre education. In 2019, he won the Hindu Playwright Award for his script *Sordid* and was chosen as a Fellow for the Arts for Good Fellowship 2019 organised by the Singapore International Foundation. He won the Sultan Padamsee Award for Playwriting 2022 for *God's Will*.

In 2022, Zero Degree Publishing published four of his plays – *The Curse of Urvashi*, *The Peacock Prince*, *Krishna's Dark Son* and *Dvijottama*. Most recently, Dhauli Books has published three of his plays – *Sordid*, *Margazhi* and *Arundhati* – as a collection.

Printed in the USA
CPSIA information can be obtained
at www.ICGtesting.com
LVHW041755301124

797921LV00009B/728